OLIVIA RODRIGO

★ ALL ACCESS ★

OLIVIA RODRIGO

Emma Carlson Berne

Scholastic Inc.

If you purchased this book without a cover, you should be aware that this book is stolen property. It was reported as "unsold and destroyed" to the publisher, and neither the author nor the publisher has received any payment for this "stripped book."

Copyright © 2025 by Scholastic Inc.

All rights reserved. Published by Scholastic Inc., *Publishers since 1920*. SCHOLASTIC and associated logos are trademarks and/or registered trademarks of Scholastic Inc.

The publisher does not have any control over and does not assume any responsibility for author or third-party websites or their content.

No part of this publication may be reproduced, stored in a retrieval system, or transmitted in any form or by any means, electronic, mechanical, photocopying, recording, or otherwise, or used to train any artificial intelligence technologies, without written permission of the publisher. For information regarding permission, write to Scholastic Inc., Attention: Permissions Department, 557 Broadway, New York, NY 10012.

This unauthorized biography was carefully researched to make sure it's accurate. This book is not sponsored by or affiliated with Ms. Rodrigo or anyone involved with her.

Photos ©: cover: Evan Agostini/Invision/AP; insert 1: Jason Kempin/Getty Images for ABA; 2 top: Rachel Murray/Getty Images for Mattel Children's Hospital UCLA; 2 bottom: Troy Harvey/ABC/Getty Images; 3: Kevin Mazur/MTV VMAs 2021/Getty Images for MTV/ViacomCBS; 4 top: Christopher Polk/Billboard via Getty Images; 4 bottom: Christopher Polk/Billboard via Getty Images; 5 left: Cindy Ord/Getty Images; 5 right: Neil Mockford/GC Images/Getty Images; 6 top: Rich Fury/Getty Images for The Recording Academy; 6 bottom: Chris Polk/Penske Media via Getty Images; 7: Frazer Harrison/Getty Images; 8: Kevin Mazur/Getty Images for The Recording Academy. All other photos © Getty Images and Shutterstock.com.

ISBN 978-1-5461-7557-5

10 9 8 7 6 5 4 3 2   25 26 27 28 29

Printed in the U.S.A.   40
First printing 2025

Series design by Sarah Salomon for The Story Division

TABLE OF CONTENTS

CHAPTER 1: *Olivia at the Wheel* — 1

CHAPTER 2: *Rocker Girl* — 9

CHAPTER 3: *On Screen* — 18

CHAPTER 4: *When It All Broke Open* — 32

CHAPTER 5: *Soaring* — 44

CHAPTER 6: *A Little Sour . . . or a Lot* — 54

CHAPTER 7: *On the Grammy Stage* — 65

CHAPTER 8: *Driving the World* — 74

CHAPTER 1

Olivia at the Wheel

The video opens with a shot of a car traveling down a lonely country road at night. Then, along with the sound of the tires on the asphalt, we hear the familiar clunks and dings of a car door opening and closing.

As the sounds continue, the first piano notes begin, and we see Olivia Rodrigo in the driver's seat, her long wavy hair spilling over her shoulders. Her face is thoughtful as she sings the now-iconic opening lines of "drivers license." "I got my driver's license last week, just like we always talked about," she sings.

Then we're out of the dark car and walking with Olivia down a sunny, ordinary suburban street with mountains in the background. She lies on the floor of a living room, wearing overalls, playing a tiny toy keyboard, serious and sad.

Olivia stands in silhouette before a boy whose face is obscured. She leans on his shoulder, stands in the middle of a parking lot illuminated by streetlights. She looks lonely. Her voice soars as she sings, "Guess you didn't mean what you wrote in the song about me," and her face crumples in tears.

Then the camera shifts as she belts out the bridge, "Red lights, stop signs, I still see your face in the white cars . . ." As the song fades, we see Olivia alone on a dark suburban cul-de-sac, her hands clasped in front of her and her hair falling around her face.

Olivia Rodrigo was only seventeen when she released "drivers license," the hit single that made her a star. In just five years, she went from newbie actor to Disney breakout star to debut singer—and now, record-breaking Grammy winner with two albums and a world tour in her rearview mirror.

Just eight years before Olivia walked the red carpet at the 2024 Grammys in a white vintage Versace gown, she was bouncing around a colorful Disney Channel set, wearing braids, cardigans, and a perky expression, playing Paige Olvera in the kids' show *Bizaardvark*. Since those early, candy-colored days, she's broken Spotify records with the release of "drivers license," filled arenas with upward of 20,000 screaming fans during her *GUTS* world tour, and stood on the Grammy Awards stage, her arms full of three golden gramophones. And she's done it all while still staying close to her mom and dad, opening up about therapy and her own mental health, and keeping media gossips away from her love life. All so she can focus on what she really considers important: her music.

Olivia has never been afraid to share her heartache in her songs. She writes about what's real and raw in her own life and in her imagination. Now her fans get a chance to ride along with her on those dark roads—and they can sing along, too!

FAST FACT

Olivia had a pet snake named Stripes when she was little. She got the snake when she was just three years old! Olivia took it to preschool one day and let everyone hold it.

THE OFFICIAL OLIVIA PLAYLIST

Get ready to get schooled! The official Olivia playlist and discography is your next study guide. Fingers crossed for an A on your exam!

☆ Olivia's first single, "All I Want," released in 2020, showed up on the *High School Musical: The Musical: The Series* soundtrack. This marked Olivia's first time on Billboard Hot 100 pop charts. The cover of the single showed her perched on a grand piano in the desert, wearing a hot pink tulle gown.

☆ "Drivers license." That's all. That's the entry. (All right, a few more details: Released as a single in January 2021, this mega-song debuted at number one on the Billboard Hot 100, where it hung out for eight weeks, eventually going platinum six times and making its creator a star.)

- Two more singles followed, "déjà vu" (April 2021) and "good 4 u" (May 2021). Both went platinum multiple times, lingering on the Billboard charts for weeks and weeks. Obviously, it was time for a . . .

- . . . debut album. SOUR came out in May 2021, laden with emotion-filled heartbreak songs that were messy, raw, and vulnerable. SOUR became the third-best-selling album of 2021, netting Olivia seven Grammy nominations and three wins.

- After SOUR's success, Olivia returned to her piano. In 2023, she released two more singles, "vampire" and "bad idea right?," both chart-toppers, both songs from her upcoming new album . . .

- GUTS, which came out on September 8, 2023. This collection was silly, angry, and edgy—more rock than pop, and more sour than sweet. Olivia's second album ate up space in the top slot of the Billboard 200 and sent her on her first world arena tour, filling 10,000 seats per show.

☆ Olivia released "get him back!" from *GUTS* as a single on September 14, 2023, and "obsessed," from the *GUTS* deluxe album, in 2024.

☆ And next up . . . fans have their fingers crossed for more great music from Olivia!

CHAPTER 2

Rocker Girl

From the moment Olivia was born, on February 20, 2003, she was immediately surrounded by music. Olivia's mom, Jennifer, was a teacher by training, but a music lover at heart. Even when Olivia was a toddler, her mom would play the '90s bands No Doubt, Smashing Pumpkins, and the White Stripes. From their home in Temecula, California, about two hours outside L.A., Jennifer would drive Olivia to her very first concert, Weezer.

Olivia absorbed her rock education like a sponge. When she was only four, she built herself a microphone stand out of Tinkertoys.

Then she sang a song she'd made up about a girl who loses her parents at the supermarket.

Her parents thought Olivia's songs were wonderful—and they thought their daughter was wonderful, too. Olivia has always described her parents as her BFFs. Even when Olivia was still in kindergarten, her parents supported her musical dreams. Music was about emotion, Olivia's mom would tell her. It was supposed to move you. The lesson stuck. When Olivia was just five years old, her parents arranged for their talented daughter to start singing lessons.

Early Talent

Jennifer Dustman, Olivia's first music teacher, realized the very first time she heard Olivia sing that her tiny student had a huge amount of talent. She arranged for Olivia to start appearing in local talent and singing competitions around town. At the age of six, Olivia took the stage at the National Association of Music Merchants trade show in Anaheim, California. Wearing two bouncy pigtails and a big black T-shirt over a long-sleeve white shirt, Olivia belted out Journey's "Don't Stop Believin'" like a future rock star. At the Boys & Girls Club Idol competition, eight-year-old Olivia sang Mötley Crüe's "Home Sweet Home."

Soon Olivia started writing her own songs, and her parents realized that learning piano would help their budding singer-songwriter. When she was nine, her dad insisted she start taking piano lessons. Olivia was *not* happy. She hated piano. She would cry before every lesson. But Jennifer and Chris wouldn't let her quit, and gradually, Olivia started writing songs to sing when she played. Her first song for piano was called "Superman," about a girl who doesn't need a hero to save her. When Jennifer Dustman heard her play it for the first time, she got chills. "I thought, 'Okay, she's a songwriter . . . That's it,'" Jennifer recalled years later.

Jennifer Dustman realized that Olivia needed even more chances to perform. And Olivia wanted to act, not just sing, especially after getting onstage as Gertrude McFuzz in the musical *Seussical*. So Jennifer convinced Olivia's parents to let her start acting classes. Soon Olivia started auditioning for small parts in TV and movies in L.A.

Olivia's mom and dad drove her ninety miles to Los Angeles—and ninety miles back. Olivia was rejected for parts over and over again. She got a little part in an Old Navy commercial, but she wanted more. And Jennifer and Chris hated the long drive. They told Olivia that she could quit trying to get acting parts if she wanted.

But Olivia didn't want to quit. She wanted to keep going. She wanted to keep going forever. And when she was ten years old, she got her chance. Olivia landed the lead role of Grace Thomas in *An American Girl: Grace Stirs Up Success*. Wearing a pink beret and brandishing a whisk for her kitchen-loving character, Olivia beamed from movie art and trailers. As Grace, she played a girl whisked off to Paris who just happens to save her grandparents' bakery and compete on a junior cooking show.

Olivia was ready for the challenge. The next chapter of her life had begun.

FAST FACT

Olivia's grandfather actually predicted her fame when she was a baby. "He held me in his arms, when I was hours old, and he was really good at zodiac things and astrology and reading charts and stuff," Olivia revealed. "And he goes, 'She's going to be a performing artist, and she's going to be really emotional.'"

SING IT! 10 SONGS OLIVIA LOVES

Olivia loves to listen to music as much as she loves to make it! Here's her playlist:

- ☆ Taylor Swift, "Picture to Burn"
- ☆ Taylor Swift, "Out of the Woods"
- ☆ Pat Benatar, "You Better Run"
- ☆ Lorde, "A World Alone"
- ☆ Billie Eilish, "My Boy"

☆ Kacey Musgraves, "Merry Go `Round"

☆ Bob Dylan, "Don't Think Twice, It's All Right"

☆ Black Sabbath, "Iron Man"

☆ Phoebe Bridgers, "Funeral"

☆ Smashing Pumpkins, "Disarm"

FAST FACT

Olivia is of Filipino heritage. Her great-grandfather emigrated from the Philippines to the United States when he was a teenager. "My dad grew up in a house where they were always making Filipino food, his grandpa always spoke Tagalog," said Olivia. "All of those traditions have trickled down to our generation."

CHAPTER 3

On Screen

Flash forward two years later. It's 2016, Olivia is twelve, and acting is her life. From the role of American Girl Grace Thomas, she's gone on to accept the part of Paige Olvera in the Disney kids' show *Bizaardvark*. On a brightly colored set, Olivia and her co-star Madison Hu play perky, quirky preteens who make funny music videos for their vlog (that's video blog to you).

Olivia was living in the world she'd wanted for so long. But her family had to live in that world, too. Now that she had to spend so much time on the *Bizaardvark* set, Jennifer and

Chris and Olivia packed up and moved their life to L.A. Olivia left behind her friends, her home, and her school. She switched to homeschooling, learned the guitar for her character, and became best friends with Madison.

On Set

For three seasons, Olivia bounced around on camera for *Bizaardvark*, wearing tight ripped jeans and elaborate hair braids. But inside, she wasn't as bouncy as her character looked. She was only a young teenager, and she was struggling to figure out what she wanted and who she really was. "Most 14-year-olds aren't in a room with adults being like, 'So, what's your brand?'" Olivia later told *Elle* magazine. She didn't know.

After three seasons and sixty-three episodes, *Bizaardvark* was canceled. Olivia immediately landed an even bigger role—her springboard, as it turned out—playing the leading role of Nini Salazar-Roberts on the Disney+ show *High School Musical: The Musical: The Series*.

Olivia loved the show immediately. The cast felt like family and friends all at the same time. Olivia starred opposite her co-star Joshua Bassett and wrote songs for her songwriting character. Nini and Joshua's character Ricky fell in love onscreen—and fans think they might have offscreen as well, though Olivia has never officially confirmed that she and Joshua were in a relationship.

Instead, Olivia preferred to focus on her acting and her songwriting. The lines between her *HSM: TM: TS* character and herself began to blur when she shared a song she wrote, "I Am More," on Instagram. Disney asked her to write another song, this time for Nini to sing on this show. In three days, Olivia created "All I Want," a love ballad, that she sang live on the set.

"All I Want" wasn't just a moment on *HSM: TM: TS*. It was a good song in its own right, and fans thought so, too. The song hit the Billboard Hot 100 pop charts. And when *HSM: TM: TS* creator Tim Federle told Olivia and co-star Joshua Bassett that they could co-write a song to sing together on the show, they were ready.

"[Olivia] and I literally turned around that minute," Joshua said later. "I grabbed my guitar, we sat down and we just started pumping out ideas. Writing it down, everything we could think of and then we'd come back every five minutes and say, 'I thought of this.'"

The process worked. Nini and Ricky, Joshua's character, performed "Just for a

Moment" on camera during the last episode of *High School Musical: The Musical: The Series*'s first season.

A New Love

Olivia still loved acting, but more and more, she was finding that she *really* loved songwriting. She adored writing songs for her characters and imagining what they might say in different situations. Even when writer's block hit—and it did, and the lyrics and tunes just wouldn't come—she didn't turn away from what was rapidly becoming her first love: music.

Olivia was still under contract with *High School Musical: The Musical: The Series*. She wasn't leaving the small screen anytime soon. But she was already thinking about what she wanted next. Many Disney kid actors had gone on to singing and movie acting careers—Miley Cyrus, Hilary Duff, Selena Gomez. Olivia began asking herself if she wanted to be like these older role models, or if she wanted to follow a different path.

FAST FACT

Olivia has always loved and admired female singer-songwriters. She bought a copy of the 1971 album Tapestry by Carole King at a thrift store when she was thirteen, and played it over and over, along with songs by Joni Mitchell and Pat Benatar.

OLIVIA ON SET

And . . . action! Both the *Bizaardvark* and *HSM: TM: TS* sets had plenty of interesting moments, both onscreen and off.

- ☆ Most of the *Bizaardvark* cast (including Olivia) went to school on the set.

- ☆ Olivia and her co-star Madison Hu each played guitar and piano and sang. At the time of filming, Olivia considered Madison the better musician, and Madison thought Olivia was a better singer.

- ☆ Cast members remember Olivia constantly singing the newest pop songs in the corridors of the set.

- ☆ The *Bizaardvark* cast would often ad-lib and improv lines during filming, which the producers frequently left in.

☆ Most of the cast of *HSM: TM: TS* had backgrounds in theater before working on the show.

☆ The costume designer for *HSM: TM: TS* made some of the jewelry the cast wore from material bought at Hobby Lobby.

☆ Because the show had so many musical performances, the cast were asked to sing songs during their auditions for the show— Olivia sang "Price Tag" by Jessie J. She also sang together with Josh Bassett.

☆ All the songs on *HSM: TM: TS* were recorded live.

OLIVIA'S FAVE NOSHES

Mmm... oatmeal with fruit, anyone? Olivia loves healthy snacks—and some comfort food once in a while, too.

- ☆ **Skinny Pop.** Olivia has said she leaves open bags of the snack around her house at all times.

- ☆ **Taco Bell's Crunchwrap.** This concoction is a flour tortilla wrapping up a crispy shell. Olivia's a vegetarian, so she orders hers with beans instead of meat (and hold the cheese and sour cream, too!).

- ☆ **Banana bread.** She makes her own and occasionally shares it with her interviewers.

- ☆ **McDonald's oatmeal.** No Egg McMuffins here! Hot oatmeal is Olivia's go-to fast-food breakfast order.

☆ **Macaroni and cheese (and bread—and a Coke).** Olivia's said that mac and cheese from the restaurant Macaroni Grill is her birthday meal every year.

☆ **Lumpias.** Olivia loves this traditional Filipino spring roll in which veggies are encased in a crispy fried wrapper. Yum!

OLIVIA'S BEST-DRESSED LIST . . .

On stages all over the world, Olivia combines sparkles, lace, boots, and leather to reflect her personality—a little punk, a little rock, a little pop.

ON TOUR . . .

☆ A pink laced corset was the centerpiece of Olivia's *SOUR* tour outfit, which also included a short pink plaid skirt, fishnet tights, and giant lace-up combat boots.

☆ Olivia referenced her song "good 4 u" with a tank top ornamented with a big heart reading "Happy and Healthy"—a line from the song—paired with a blue plaid pleated skirt and her favorite fishnet tights.

- ☆ Olivia owned the stage on her GUTS tour in a white tank, sparkly blue briefs, sparkly star-patterned tights, and combat boots to top off the punk-meets-cute look.

- ☆ With a backdrop of a giant pair of lips, Olivia matched those kissers with a lipstick-red sparkly bodysuit and black tights.

- ☆ For an edgy look, Olivia dropped a sheer chainmail dress over a shiny black bikini top and high-waisted matching shorts, rounding out the look with torn black fishnet tights.

. . . AND ON THE GRAMMY STAGE

- ☆ Olivia embraced a vamp vibe for the 2022 Grammys when she walked the red carpet in a black, floor-length gown with body-outline crystals, plus a choker and long black gloves.

- ☆ To present at the 2023 Grammys, Olivia stepped out in a sheer black gown with a visible bra and short-shorts outfit underneath. She kept her jewelry simple and wore a black necklace with one giant bead.

 For the 2024 Grammys, Olivia went vintage in a white gown studded with red beads that had been originally worn by supermodel Linda Evangelista in 1995.

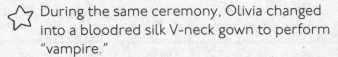 During the same ceremony, Olivia changed into a bloodred silk V-neck gown to perform "vampire."

CHAPTER 4

When It All Broke Open

"All I Want" quickly racked up over 200 million global streams. Olivia was only seventeen, but she was ready to make a big decision—she wanted to pursue her music career. She was ready for a record deal.

Olivia started meeting with different record labels. She knew that other Disney kid stars had gone with Disney's own record label. But Olivia wanted to be a singer-songwriter and make her own music—something that other Disney kid actors had not done. She wanted to have her own unique voice. When she met with the executives at Geffen Records, they talked to her about how much they liked her songwriting skills, not just her star power. Olivia liked that. "I want to be a songwriter," she told *The Guardian* newspaper in an interview. "I don't want to be the biggest pop star that ever lived."

COVID Times

Olivia got her chance to buckle down to songwriting when the COVID-19 pandemic swept the world in March 2020. Olivia had just gotten her driver's license. She would drive around in the dark on her own, feeling especially independent. In a car, Olivia said later, you're alone. No one can hear you. You're isolated, but you're also free.

Olivia listened to emotional songs and she'd think about the relationship she'd been in—the one she sings about in "drivers license." Sometimes, she'd cry. As she explained later on TikTok, when she got home, she thought that lonely, nighttime melancholy might make a good song.

Olivia sat down at the piano and cried and wrote. She channeled her feelings into a kind of creative magic that eventually turned into the biggest hit of her life. She and her producer recorded sounds from her mom's own car. Then, they put it all together in the studio.

On January 8, 2021, Olivia released her single "drivers license." Within a week, the song was streamed over 76 million times in the United States alone. It became the first song of 2021 to have one billion streams, and it climbed to number one on the Billboard Hot 100, making Olivia the youngest person to top the Billboard chart. "It's been the absolute craziest week of my life," Olivia told the *New York Times* during the "drivers license" release. "My entire life just, like, shifted in an instant."

She remembered calling her record label representative on FaceTime while she sat in a grocery store parking lot in Utah. "Drivers license" was in the top slot on Apple Music. "We were looking at each other on FaceTime, speechless," Olivia told *Variety*. "[And] just stared at each other for a minute. 'What do we do?' 'I don't know.' That was the moment that I knew that it was going to be something bigger than I expected."

Praise from music critics flooded in. *Rolling Stone* called it "potent" and asked, "Is it too early to call song of the year?" The *New York Times* music critic said, "Now that's a bridge!" The *Los Angeles Times* called it a "swooning power ballad."

Olivia knew she'd hit the big time when *Saturday Night Live* aired a skit about "drivers license." On the show, a bunch of grown men hear the song as they're playing pool, and they pretend they don't know much about it—until the melody grabs them and they start singing along and crying. "DRIVERS LICENSE SNL SKETCH IS THE BEST BIRTHDAY PRESENT EVER IM SHAKING," Olivia wrote on Twitter.

Three months after that skit aired, Olivia herself appeared on the *Saturday Night Live* stage, in a pink dress studded with darker pink crystals, her waist-length wavy hair cascading over her shoulders. She was so nervous backstage before performing that she was shaking and crying—and wondering if she could even go on. But Dan Nigro, her producer, was there in the dressing room with her. He told Olivia that he believed in her and that he knew she could go on and perform. She did—and the audience loved it.

Love Triangle

But people weren't just interested in "drivers license" for its haunting lyrics and beautiful video. The song also left fans wondering. Was "drivers license" really about a love triangle between Olivia and her *HSM: TM: TS* co-stars Joshua Bassett and Sabrina Carpenter? Sabrina was blonde, and she was older than Olivia, just like in the song lyrics. And both Joshua and Sabrina released songs of their own that seemed to answer "drivers license." In Joshua's song "Lie, Lie, Lie," he sings about a girl who can't get him off her mind, and the music video shows him driving alone in a car, too. Was that a call-out to "drivers license?" Sabrina's song "Skin" talks about not letting someone get under her skin—perhaps Olivia?

But Olivia, Joshua, and Sabrina have never confirmed or denied that Olivia and Joshua were involved. They haven't said who their songs were about. "I don't really subscribe to hating other women because of boys," Olivia told *Variety* in an interview. "I think that's so stupid, and I really resent that narrative that was being tossed around." She's also pointed out that these rumors are actually the least important part of the song. She wants her fans to focus on the music and the emotions and the beauty of the lyrics.

FAST FACT

Olivia visited the White House during the COVID-19 pandemic and promoted vaccination among young people. She got to meet President Biden and his chief medical adviser, Dr. Fauci; toured the West Wing; and addressed the press from the briefing room's podium.

OLIVIA TAKES THE STAGE . . .

Olivia's gotten used to gracing stages all over the world. Here's a few of her best moments:

☆ Olivia unofficially became a superstar when she appeared as the musical guest on *Saturday Night Live* in 2021. In her pink dotted dress, she performed "drivers license," and later "good 4 u" in a plaid pantsuit.

☆ Olivia left it all onstage when she performed "vampire" at the 2024 Grammys. At one point during the song, fake blood started trickling from her hand down her arm and from the backdrop behind her. By the end of the song, her cheeks were smeared with blood.

☆ When props started falling over during Olivia's performance of "vampire" at the 2023 MTV Video Music Awards, she had to leave the stage without finishing the song. A minute later, she was back with a surprise performance of "get him back!"

☆ Olivia paid homage to one of pop's greats when she performed Carly Simon's "You're So Vain" in honor of the singer's introduction into the Rock & Roll Hall of Fame in 2022.

☆ Olivia's "stage" was actually an empty DMV office when she performed one of National Public Radio's Tiny Desk (Home) Concerts under 2021 COVID-19-era pandemic restrictions.

BEST FAN MOMENTS

Olivia's silliest and cutest moments onstage and off!

☆ During a March 2024 *GUTS* tour concert, Olivia asked a fan if it was her birthday. When the woman said it was, Olivia sang her "Happy Birthday." But she didn't know the fan's name, so she substituted, "Pretty Girl in a Pink Dress."

☆ During an April 2022 concert, Olivia said she wanted to kiss someone, so her cameraman pointed out a group of young men. Olivia picked one and kissed him on the hand!

☆ Movie stars Tobey Maguire and Adam Sandler showed up at one of Olivia's L.A. shows. Adam Sandler brought his kids, then took a video as they danced and sang along to Olivia's music.

☆ Olivia often hops down off the stage and mingles with fans in the front rows of her show, shaking their hands and offering selfies.

☆ When Olivia met an awestruck fan outside the *Today* show in 2023, the girl started crying as she hugged Olivia. Olivia told her she liked her outfit, then posed for a selfie.

CHAPTER 5

Soaring

For most folks, having your song break the pop world might be enough for one year. But not for Olivia. After she released "drivers license" in January 2021, she graduated from high school—on Instagram, she shared a casual photo of herself in a blue cap and gown, flashing the peace sign. She also moved out of her parents' apartment and into her own for the very first time—although she pointed out that even though she had her own address, she was over at her parents' house and they were at hers so much that she wasn't really living on her own. And she liked it that way. Olivia didn't have a lot of experience buying her own groceries or keeping her place clean. She needed to practice some first.

Olivia was still as close as ever to Jennifer and Chris. She plays all her songs for her mom first, and she trusts Jennifer's opinion. "If my mom doesn't like it, I know it's not music that makes you feel," Olivia told *Teen Vogue*. In fact, when Olivia played the bridge for "drivers license" for her mom, Jennifer told her daughter that the melody sounded odd and didn't fit with the rest of the song!

Taking Care of Herself

"Drivers license" had made Olivia a star, but she also struggled with her image on social media and the comments she encountered. She's not blonde and blue-eyed, Olivia has pointed out.

She's Filipina American, and she's proud of her heritage. But she found it hard not to compare herself to blonde, blue-eyed girls who looked more stereotypically all-American.

Olivia has realized how overwhelming social media can be. "You can create your own reality sometimes with social media . . . What you see just becomes your reality, and it's totally not at all," she said in an interview with *The Guardian*. She's taken steps to guard her mental health—like talking with a therapist, which she's done since she was sixteen. She's cut back on her social media time, and made sure her schedule has time for resting, being alone, and being with her friends—*without* talking about music or the music world! And she tries to remember what her mom says: "Those who matter don't mind, and those who mind don't matter."

Olivia's confidence in her voice soared after "drivers license." She was ready for more. The

COVID-19 lockdown gave her the perfect chance to write more songs. Olivia promised herself she'd write one song per day while she was sheltering at home. She thought the pandemic might last two weeks. It lasted much, much longer, but for almost six months, Olivia did write one song per day! She poured her feelings of loneliness and isolation into her melodies and lyrics, and soon, she had put together *SOUR*. Originally, she and her label planned to release this new collection as an EP—a group of songs that's not quite as long or put-together as an album. But Olivia told her label that she wanted to put out a full-length album. Okay, they told her. If you're willing to work for it.

Worker Bee

She was. She chose producer Daniel Nigro to help her—not because he loved her music so much, but because he was the first producer to tell her that her songs weren't good enough. That's what Olivia wanted—honesty.

So Olivia got to work. Seven days a week for thirteen hours a day, she and Daniel recorded the songs that would make up *SOUR*. Dan said later that Olivia was one of the hardest workers he'd met in a studio. Olivia never wanted to just do a few tries on a song and then trust that Dan could fix it in editing later. Instead, she wanted to try different versions over and over—sometimes dozens of times.

Olivia honored what her mother had taught her—that music should make you feel, even if those feelings are intense. "Something I'm really proud of is that this record talks about emotions that are hard to talk about or aren't really socially acceptable, especially for girls," Olivia said in an

OLIVIA'S RELATIONSHIP TIMELINE

Olivia tries to keep her relationships grounded, real, and drama-free.

 Ethan Wacker, 2018
Olivia's early romance with *Bizaardvark* co-star Ethan Wacker was short and sweet. The two took pictures of themselves by a Los Angeles swimming pool and in matching tracksuits and posted the snaps to social media. After the relationship ended, they remained friends and Olivia wished Ethan good thoughts when he went off to college.

Josh Basset, 2019–2020
Olivia and Josh were fictional love interests in *HSM: TM: TS*, and while they never publicly said they were dating, the two seemed to be in a relationship. Josh wrote several songs apparently about Olivia—and of course, fans have wondered if "drivers license" is about Josh and their co-star Sabrina Carpenter.

 Adam Faze, 2021–2022
Olivia and producer Adam Faze were together at a premiere for the movie *Space Jam 2*, at the Six Flags amusement park, and afterward, spent time together in Los Angeles. They kept their relationship mostly private, though some fans think that the song "vampire" might be about Adam. Olivia has not confirmed or denied!

 Zack Bia, 2022
Olivia started going out with DJ and producer Zack Bia around Super Bowl time, after breaking up with Adam Faze. Zack invited Olivia to a few Super Bowl parties that he was DJing. They dated casually for a few months before drifting apart but staying friends.

interview. "[Anger], jealousy, spite, sadness, they're frowned-upon as . . . moaning and complaining or whatever. But I think they're such valid emotions."

FAST FACT

Olivia started seeing a therapist when she was sixteen, at the recommendation of her therapist dad. She's said that the mental health support helps her deal with the stresses of her job.

Louis Partridge, 2023–Now!

Actor Louis and Olivia first got together in December 2023. Olivia traveled to England to visit Louis and his friends, and Louis went to Olivia's *Saturday Night Live* taping and has shown up in the audience during her *GUTS* tour stops. Louis has even helped Olivia shoot TikToks announcing further *GUTS* tour dates—proof of a supportive boyfriend.

CHAPTER 6

A Little Sour . . . or a Lot

On April 13, 2021, Olivia posted a picture of herself on Twitter with her arms crossed and her unsmiling face covered with bright stickers. She's sticking out her tongue, which sports letter stickers spelling out S-O-U-R. "My debut album *SOUR* out May 21st ahhh," she tweeted. A second picture showed a pearl-colored balloon with the album tracks printed on it. A hand reaches out with an open safety pin from the side of the picture, ready to pop it.

All of Olivia's hard work was about to pay off. *SOUR* debuted in May, as Olivia had promised, with the Twitter pictures as the album's front and back cover. *SOUR* had the biggest opening week sales on Spotify of any album by a female artist in 2021. It topped *Rolling Stone*'s list of 50 Best Albums of 2021—and within a year, it went triple platinum. The album sat on the list of Top 10 US Albums of the Century longer than any other album—eventually surpassing Lady Gaga's *The Fame*, which had previously held the record.

Writing for Herself

Olivia was there for it. Even though a lot of the songs were about heartbreak, she was happy when she was writing them, she said. She wanted to connect with her fans and with other teenagers who were feeling the same powerful emotions that she was.

But Olivia was worried about one thing, she said. Maybe these songs would be hard for other kids to relate to. After all, she'd pretty much grown up on TV sets. That wasn't a typical childhood or adolescence. But she didn't need to worry. Olivia's fans felt seen and heard. They felt like she understood them. "I always write my songs for me. I don't write them for anyone else," Olivia told *People* magazine. "What I put out into the world, I try to remember that I did everything I wanted to do . . . And how people perceive it, or speculate about who it's about or whatever, that really just has nothing to do with me. My only job is to write songs that I really love, and that's what I try to work from."

Olivia doesn't forget either that she's helping to represent Filipino Americans, too.

Even though she didn't think much about being Filipina growing up—she went to school with lots of kids from diverse ethnic backgrounds—she loves thinking about inspiring other Asian American children and being an example for them.

Olivia also doesn't mind pushing back against critics who say that she only writes about heartbreak. She's pointed out that a male songwriter wouldn't be criticized for his song subjects. "I feel like if a girl writes a song about heartbreak, very often people start criticizing her for feeling those emotions, and only writing about that. I do just love a heartbreak song," Olivia said in an interview. "I literally wrote breakup songs before I ever held a boy's hand. So, who knows? Maybe I'll continue to do that, or maybe I'll branch out? I just love writing music, and I hope that people continue to listen."

Adam on the Scene

One fan in particular was listening—music producer Adam Faze. Olivia and Adam met through mutual music friends and started dating during the summer of 2021. They went public with their romance at the premiere of the movie *Space Jam 2* at the Six Flags amusement park in California. But even though Olivia introduced Adam to the media as her boyfriend and was photographed out with him a few times, she preferred to keep her relationship private. She didn't post on social media about Adam, and when they broke up in early 2022, she also kept her relationship status quiet.

Other changes were coming, too. Olivia had committed to working out her contract with *High School Musical: The Musical: The Series* through the three seasons she'd promised. But now, in 2022, her contract was up.

A young Olivia with her best friend and co-star MADISON HU.

Olivia smiles for the camera with her co-stars on *HSM: TM: TS*.

Performing "good 4 u" at the 2021 MTV Video Music Awards.

Olivia doesn't forget her DOC MARTENS onstage at a *GUTS* show.

PURPLE is Olivia's favorite color. "I like it," she says. "It's the color of magic and all things mystic." Even her guitar is purple!

Olivia is stunning at the GOVERNORS AWARDS in January 2024.

Olivia sang her heart out during her performance of "vampire" at the 2024 Grammys.

And with the wild success of *SOUR*, she was ready to leave TV acting behind (along with Adam Faze), and fully embrace her new life as a singer-songwriter.

FAST FACT

Days before SOUR's debut, Taylor Swift expressed her support for Olivia by sending her a ring similar to the one she herself had worn when she wrote Red.

OLIVIA LOVES . . .

SO many random things. Like . . .

⭐ **Her mom!** Olivia's said in many interviews that they are BFFs—and Jennifer has helped influence Olivia's musical tastes. "Her favorite music is punk music and metal music and really hard, gritty stuff, so she's always been the one that has instilled in me that, 'I don't care [about] the technicalities—if it makes you feel something, then it's good music,'" Olivia told *Teen Vogue*.

⭐ **Vintage clothes.** Olivia not only wowed at the 2024 Grammys in a white vintage gown, she's also worn a 1995 gold sequined miniskirt while promoting *GUTS*, a 1990s slip dress to a *SOUR* party, and a pink 2001 gown to the 2021 MTV VMAs.

☆ **Green living.** Olivia's spoken up about her belief in green and sustainable living, especially when it comes to fashion. She no longer buys new clothes and wears them once like she used to, she's said. Now, she rewears clothes, wears vintage or thrifted clothes, or buys from brands that use sustainable practices.

☆ **Her gray-and-white kitty, Kumo,** who sometimes likes to sleep under the covers with her.

☆ **Her friends.** Former co-star Madison Hu, fellow singer Billie Eilish, and actor Iris Apatow are among Olivia's closest supports. She and Iris even have matching heart tattoos on their fingers.

OLIVIA'S MUSICAL MUSES

Olivia's always ready to talk about the musicians who have inspired her to write, sing—and keep going.

- ☆ **Avril Lavigne**—Olivia told an audience how much she admires the "Sk8er Boi" singer.

- ☆ **The Killers**—The alt-rock band's single "Somebody Told Me" is one of Olivia's favorites.

- ☆ **Alanis Morrissette**—Olivia has told interviewers that Morrissette's hit album *Jagged Little Pill* inspired her to look at singing and songwriting in a brand-new way.

- ☆ **One Direction**—Confession! Olivia used to write One Direction fan fiction when she was in middle school.

☆ **Taylor Swift**—Fans have noticed how much Olivia's song "déjà vu" has in common with Taylor's "Cruel Summer," and Olivia is proud to claim that Taylor's song directly inspired her.

☆ **Lorde**—The New Zealand singer-songwriter's music encouraged Olivia to think of her own music as art.

☆ **Katy Perry**—The pop superstar was a mentor to Olivia, and she closes GUTS with "teenage dream"—the same title as Perry's hit single.

CHAPTER 7

On the Grammy Stage

On April 3, 2022, Olivia stood onstage at the MGM Grand Garden Arena in Las Vegas in a shape-hugging black gown with glittering purple accents and long black gloves. Tears were already in her eyes as she hugged the Grammy she'd just won for Best New Artist. "Whoa, oh god, thank you so much to the recording academy, this is my biggest dream come true," she said, her voice choked up. "Thank you to my amazing parents and best friends, Iris, Maddie, and Conan, I love you guys, and huge thanks to Dan, who made all my music with me."

Beaming, she made her way off-stage, but she would be back in front of the microphone twice more that night. In addition to performing "drivers license," Olivia won three of the seven categories in which she was nominated. In addition to Best New Artist, she carried home gold gramophones for Best Pop Vocal Album for *SOUR* and Best Pop Solo Performance for "drivers license." Jennifer and Chris were there in the audience, watching and beaming along with her new boyfriend, producer and DJ Zack Bia. Olivia told the crowd, "When I was nine years old, I told my mom I was going to be an Olympic gymnast even though I could barely do a cartwheel, and she thought I was joking, and I got super defensive. And so the next week when I told her I was going to win a Grammy she was very supportive, even though I'm sure she thought it was just a little kid pipe dream . . . I want to thank my mom and my dad for being equally as proud of me for winning a Grammy as they were when I learned how to do a back walkover. This is for you guys, and because of you guys."

Olivia's momentum showed no signs of slowing down after the Grammys. She met with the director of the *Hunger Games* prequel, *The Ballad of Songbirds and Snakes*, to talk about writing and performing a song for the movie's closing credits. The movie's director, Francis Lawrence, talked to Olivia for almost an hour during their meeting, telling her all about the movie's themes, and even though he later said he was embarrassed for going on and on, Olivia didn't seem to mind. She took a lot of notes, and in the end, her song, "Can't Catch Me Now," was exactly what Francis was hoping for.

From the GUT(S)

Olivia was busy with other songs, too—mainly, her new album, *GUTS*. For a year and half, she'd been writing songs. She was excited to make a new album, but first she had to fight the voices in her head—the voices of all the people who expected her to reproduce her *SOUR* success. Could she do it? Would she let her fans down? After all, she wasn't the same person she'd been when she wrote *SOUR*. "Oh, my god, I'm not a seventeen-year-old girl going through her first heartbreak anymore," Olivia said, recalling the person she was while writing *GUTS*. "That's such a universally relatable experience. How am I going to make something that people can get behind?"

She was feeling a lot of pressure, but as time went on, Olivia was able to relax and start writing the songs she wanted to hear out there in the world. After all, she told herself, she'd already achieved everything she wanted—and she was only nineteen! Now she could let go and write songs just for herself.

GUTS came out on September 8, 2023. Critics called it a little cheeky, a little playful, and a lot punk. It was filled with tracks that Olivia said were very personal. Some were angry anthems. "Vampire" screamed, "The way you sold me for parts . . . as you sunk your teeth into me, oh." Olivia wasn't afraid to be angry instead of sad. She was only afraid of not being herself.

FAST FACT

Rocker Courtney Love accused Olivia of copying the cover of her 1994 album *Hole* when Olivia released a promo picture of herself dressed as a prom queen, holding a bouquet of flowers and crying. Olivia responded, "To be honest, I'm just flattered that Courtney Love knows that I exist."

TALKING ABOUT OLIVIA

Olivia's followers and fellow celebrities are always glad to share their thoughts on their favorite heartbreak queen.

 "She's so effortless when it comes to lyric writing it's pretty incredible to witness," says Nigro. "Sometimes she'll run a line by me, and I'll help her tweak it to make it stronger. But most of the time she's just running with it."
—**Producer Dan Nigro**

"She's incredible and I am such a fan of hers. I love her music and it's amazing seeing it continue to live on."
—**Actor and former *High School Musical* star Vanessa Hudgens**

"Man, she's super talented, super young, and able to speak to these things that are sort of these big, universal themes."
—Nick Jonas

 "Rare is the artist who can transport that way, especially at such a young age. And for anyone going through their first heartbreak, Olivia's voice is a light in the dark, a promise that your pain can someday become a deep source of power."
—Gwen Stefani

 "I remember first hearing ['drivers license'] and being like, 'This is an incredible tune,' and then finding out she was like seventeen . . . That was the age when I started writing songs, and I did not write a song of that caliber. I couldn't sing at that caliber either . . . She's an extreme talent. She's a very special artist. Very special."
—Ed Sheeran

FAST FACT

Pilates is one of Olivia's favorite workout routines. She makes time for it even when she's on tour, and has been spotted at Pilates studios as far from home as Birmingham, in the United Kingdom!

CHAPTER 8

Driving the World

The screaming arena was dark and filled with the lights of cell phones. Behind the stage, giant red patterns swirled and resolved into photos of Olivia and vinyl records. Olivia stalked to the middle of the stage, clad in a shiny red bodysuit. Her black hair flowed over her shoulders as she sang into her microphone, staring out intensely at the audience. It was February 23, 2024, and Olivia was at the Acrisure Arena in Palm Springs, California. Two weeks earlier, she'd performed "vampire" onstage at the 2024 Grammys. She didn't snare any awards—but now she was kicking off her *GUTS* world tour—and the arenas she had booked were already selling out.

Growing Up

Olivia's songs focused on independence and controlling her own life. She was growing up, she told her audience that night in Palm Springs. She'd just turned twenty-one. And she was excited—and maybe a little scared. She was still young, though, and she could still be silly. Even the concert poster for *GUTS* tapped into her playful, goofy side. A surprised-looking Olivia has her mouth open, as if she is vomiting the star-surrounded words "*GUTS* World Tour," while an unseen person's hand holds her hair back. During the show, Olivia danced around with a big *L* up to her forehead and held up a big red megaphone with her mic stuck in the waistband of her pants.

But Olivia's vibe during her *GUTS* opening show wasn't all silly. During the song "brutal," she sank to the floor while playing her guitar. She grabbed a drummer's stick out of his hand and banged the drums a couple times herself. She asked the audience to think of someone who had made them mad—then scream as loud as they could while all the lights in the arena turned off.

Olivia's tour just keeps going. In addition to her forty-eight North American tour stops, she added stops in Europe, Asia, and Australia, bringing her global shows up to ninety-four. In October 2024, the *GUTS* tour finally wrapped up in Sydney, Australia.

Supporting Her Causes

But Olivia makes sure that she leaves her mark *off* the stage as well as on it—and she makes sure the world knows which causes she supports and what she believes in. For the North American leg of her tour, she partnered with a prominent women's health organization, and donated part of her ticket sales. She's started Olivia Rodrigo's Fund 4 Good, which also promotes reproductive health freedom around the world for women and girls. And in different regions of the world, Olivia supports different nonprofits working to help women. In Canada, she donated to a group that runs shelters for women fleeing violence. In Europe, Olivia linked with WAVE (Women Against Violence Europe).

When *Rolling Stone* released its list of 500 Greatest Songs of All Time on February 16, 2024, "drivers license" stood at number 377. Olivia has three Grammys, two platinum-selling albums, and a world arena tour to check off her "To-Do Before 22" list. And she's told *Variety* recently that her acting career is far from over. "I just love telling stories, whether that be in a song or movie, that's really something that really excites me," she said. And while this überstar rock princess hasn't said anything about new music yet, she definitely plans to keep writing. All her fans—and the world—have to do is wait. Olivia Rodrigo is just getting started.

FAST FACT

Olivia owns the master recordings of her songs. She made sure that was written into her record contract, and has said she was inspired to protect her music by Taylor Swift.

OLIVIA HELPS

Olivia's always reaching out a hand of support to organizations and causes she believes in—and to her fans!

☆ Olivia started her Fund 4 Good to support reproductive health for women and girls. She donates part of her *GUTS* ticket sales to the fund.

☆ During her Canadian *GUTS* tour, Olivia donated to a system of shelters for women and children who are fleeing violence.

☆ Olivia reached out to the European group WAVE (Women Against Violence Europe) when she was on tour for *GUTS* across the Atlantic. The group also supports women who are affected by violence.

☆ Olivia has helped to raise millions of dollars for the Epidermolysis Bullosa Research Partnership, which helps raise research funds for people afflicted with a rare skin disease.

IN HER OWN WORDS

Olivia's never shy about sharing her thoughts on writing, love, emotions, and of course, making music.

☆ "I always loved songwriting. That was my first love, my first passion when I was so young. I remember being four years old or something, and making up all these crazy songs about my four-year-old problems."

☆ "It was an incredible experience to write a song ['drivers license'] that you feel accurately expresses intense heartbreak, pain and longing, and watch all of those sad feelings resonate with other people."

☆ "I love criticism, honestly . . . I think I can grow so much from people being like, 'Oh, I wish it was more like this,' and I'm like, 'Oh cool . . . I'm learning.'"

☆ "I'm comfortable being vulnerable with people, and many times people associate vulnerability with weakness. From a young age, I realized that vulnerability equates to strength, and that's so true in my songwriting."

☆ "I definitely talked about my deepest, darkest secrets and insecurities on *SOUR*—which is sort of strange to be like, 'Here, you guys can have this. Anyone who wants to listen to it can listen to it . . .' But it's really empowering when it comes out, and it's been really awesome for me to see people resonate with that vulnerability and relate to it."

☆ "My parents take all this craziness in the best way. They always say, 'We are so proud of you and all these achievements are incredible, but we would be equally proud of you if you were in school in your hometown.' They're the best and that's a really important attitude to have."

☆ "It's so nice to be welcomed into the music industry and so great to be supportive of other women . . . [Taylor Swift] wrote me a letter a while ago, and she wrote something about how you make your own luck in the world, and how you treat other people always comes back to you."

☆ "I think that I am very multifaceted as a person, and some days I feel like I want to be super sarcastic and satirical and I feel angry and pissed. And, other times, I'm feeling really sentimental and want to write a guitar ballad. I think that it's fun to play with different aspects of your personality, but I always try to make it seem genuine and true to who I am on a soul level, too."

FAST FACT

Olivia sells some of her own clothes and clothes from her music videos in an online shop, then donates the money to charity.

AN OLIVIA TIMELINE

February 2024

"Drivers license" appears at number 377 on *Rolling Stone*'s list of 500 Greatest Songs of All Time on February 16, 2024. Olivia performs at the 2024 Grammys. Olivia kicks off her GUTS world tour.

September 8, 2023

GUTS, Olivia's second album, is released.

2023

Olivia records "Can't Catch Me Now" for the *Hunger Games* prequel, *The Ballad of Songbirds and Snakes*.

April 2022

Olivia wins three Grammys (Best New Artist, Best Pop Vocal Album, Best Pop Solo Performance).

September 2021

Olivia makes her first appearance at a major American music awards show, performing "good 4 u" at the MTV Video Music Awards.

July 2021

Olivia visits the White House to promote COVID-19 vaccination among young people.

June 2021

Olivia graduates from high school.

May 2021

Olivia's debut album, *SOUR*, is released and becomes the third-best-selling album of the year. Olivia performs on *Saturday Night Live*.

February 20, 2021

Saturday Night Live parodies "drivers license" in a skit, signaling the song's popularity.

January 8, 2021

Olivia releases "drivers license," which becomes a global smash hit. Within one week, the song was streamed 76 million times.

2020

Olivia writes the love ballad "All I Want" at the request of *High School*

Musical: The Musical: The Series producers, and the song lands on the Billboard charts at number 90.

2019

After *Bizaardvark* is canceled, Olivia is cast as Nini in *High School Musical: The Musical: The Series*.

2016

Olivia is cast as Paige Olvera in Disney's *Bizaardvark*. Olivia and her family move to Los Angeles.

2015

After auditioning, Olivia lands her first movie role as Grace in *An American Girl: Grace Stirs Up Success*.

2010

Olivia sings "Don't Stop Believin'" at the National Association of Music Merchants trade show in Anaheim, California.

2008

Olivia begins private singing lessons at the age of five.

February 20, 2003

Olivia is born in Murrieta, California.